To _____

From _____

God made the sun,
   He made the sky,
He made the trees
   and birds that fly.
God made the flowers,
   He made the light,
He made the stars
   that shine at night.
God made the rain,
   He made the dew,
And He made a
   special friend like you!

The Helen Steiner Rice Foundation

Whatever the celebration, whatever the day, whatever the event, whatever the occasion, Helen Steiner Rice possessed the ability to express the appropriate feeling for that particular moment.

A happening became happier, a sentiment more sentimental, a memory more memorable because of her deep sensitivity and ability to put into understandable language the emotion being experienced. Her positive attitude, her concern for others, and her love of God are identifiable threads woven into her life, her work . . . and even her death.

Prior to her passing, she established the Helen Steiner Rice Foundation, a nonprofit corporation whose purpose is to award grants to worthy charitable programs that aid the elderly, the needy, and the poor. In her lifetime, these were the individuals about whom Mrs. Rice was greatly concerned.

Royalties from the sale of this book will add to the financial capabilities of the Helen Steiner Rice Foundation, thus making possible additional grants to various qualified, worthwhile, and charitable programs. Because of her foresight, her caring, and her deep convictions, Helen Steiner Rice continues to touch a countless number of lives. Thank you for your assistance in helping to keep Helen's dreams alive.

The Helen Steiner Rice Foundation

John Ruthven, internationally acknowledged master of wildlife art, has won numerous national and international awards for his paintings. The founder of Wildlife Internationale, Inc., he has won the prestigious Federal Duck Stamp design competition.

Wings of Encouragement

Poems by

HELEN STEINER RICE

Paintings by

JOHN A. RUTHVEN

Compiled by **Virginia J. Ruehlmann**

Fleming H. Revell
A Division of Baker Book House Co
Grand Rapids, Michigan 49516

Published by Fleming H. Revell
a division of Baker Book House Company
P.O. Box 6287, Grand Rapids, MI 49516-6287

Third printing, September 1998

Printed in the United States of America

Library of Congress Cataloging-in-Publication Data

Rice, Helen Steiner.
    Wings of encouragement / poems by Helen Steiner Rice ;
paintings by John A. Ruthven ; compiled by Virginia J.
Ruehlmann.
        p.   cm.
    ISBN 0-8007-1704-X
    1. Christian poetry, American. 2. Birds—Poetry. I.
Ruthven, John A. II. Ruehlmann, Virginia J. III. Title.
PS3568.I28W56   1995
811'.54—dc20   94-46001

For current information about all releases from Baker Book
House, visit our web site:
            http://www.bakerbooks.com

Contents

to all who
find encouragement in
reading inspirational poetry and
in studying God's feathered friends,
and to all who offer
encouragement with
a smile, a song, a word, or an action.

Introduction

From the gardens of private residences to trees and green spaces in public parks, from birdhouses in backyards to tall buildings on city streets, from the muddy banks of rivers and lakes to sandy shores of seas and oceans, from treeless prairies, grassy meadows, crop or cattle farmlands to snowcapped mountains, from the dry, parched deserts to the evergreen, deciduous, and rain forests . . . birds of all kinds can be found!

Even a casual observer is fascinated with the variety of colors, songs, and interesting characteristics of our feathered friends.

Bird-watching or birding is one of the most popular of our national pastimes.

Birds are easy to observe in their natural habitats. Many are attired in vibrantly colored plumage. Their natural finery far exceeds that of an elegant fashion show. Birds also serve as valuable indicators of changes in and the quality of the weather and the environment. We all can enjoy their musical communication.

The meaningful words of poet Helen Steiner Rice and the realistic works of talented artist John A. Ruthven show their appreciation for the beauty and inspiration found in birds. May this book, which combines the God-given gifts of these two remarkable individuals, hearten you in your everyday life and assist you to inspire others.

Encouragingly,
Virginia J. Ruehlmann

Bald Eagle

Courage—Bald Eagle

Saw my white-headed eagle again. . . . It was a fine sight, he is mainly—i.e. his wings and body—so black against the sky, and they contrast so strongly with his white head and tail. He was first flying low over the water, then rose gracefully and circled westward toward White Pond. Lying on the ground with my glass, I could watch him easily, and by turns he gave me all possible views of himself. . . . He rose very high at least, till I almost lost him in the clouds, circling or rather looping along westward, high over the river and wood and farm, effectually concealed in the sky. We who live this plodding life here below never know how many eagles fly over us.

Thoreau

With an average weight of ten to thirteen pounds and a body about three feet long, the bald eagle is the largest hunting bird on the North American continent. Because of its superb vision, large wings, powerful feet, sharp talons, and curved beak, the eagle is adept at spotting, catching, and consuming fish.

Bald Eagle

Storms Bring Out the Eagles

I say to myself
    as threatening clouds hover—
Don't fold up your wings
    and run for cover,
But, like the eagle,
    spread wide your wings
And soar far above
    the troubles life brings.
For the eagle knows
    that the higher he flies
The more tranquil and brighter
    become the skies.
There is nothing in life
    God ever asks us to bear
That we can't soar above
    on the wings of prayer.
And in looking back over
    the storm you passed through,
You'll find you gained strength
    and new courage, too,
For in facing life's storms
    with an eagle's wings,
You can fly far above
    earth's small, petty things.

Bald Eagle

Let Daily Prayers Dissolve Your Cares

We all have cares and problems
    we cannot solve alone,
But if we go to God in prayer,
    we are never on our own,
And if we try to stand alone,
    we are weak and we will fall,
For God is always greatest
    when we're helpless, lost and small.

So meet Him in the morning
    and go with Him through the day
And thank Him for His guidance
    each evening when you pray.
For, like a soaring eagle,
    you too can rise above
The storms of life around you
    on the wings of prayer and love.

Bald Eagle

Help Us to See and Understand

God, give us wider vision
    to see and understand
That both the sunshine and the showers
    are gifts from Thy great hand.

Teach us that it takes the shower
    to make the flowers grow,
And only in the storms of life
    when the winds of trouble blow

Can man too reach maturity
    and grow in faith and grace
And gain the strength and courage
    to enable him to face

Sunny days as well as rain,
    high peaks as well as low,
Knowing that the April showers
    make May flowers grow.

And then at last may we accept
    the sunshine and the showers,
Confident it takes them both
    to make salvation ours.

Eastern Bluebird

Happiness—Bluebird

And yonder bluebird with the earth tinge on his breast and the sky tinge on his back—did he come down out of heaven on that bright March morning when he told us so softly and plaintively that, if we pleased, spring had come? Indeed, there is nothing in the return of the birds more curious and suggestive than in the first appearance, or rumors of the appearance, of this little blue-coat. The bird at first seems a mere wandering voice in the air; . . . its call . . . falls like a drop of rain when no cloud is visible; one looks and listens, but to no purpose. The weather changes, perhaps a cold snap with snow comes on, and it may be a week before I hear the note again, and this time or the next perchance see the bird sitting on a stake in the fence lifting his wing as he calls cheerily to his mate.

John Burroughs (1895)

Since fruit orchards and natural tree cavities are quickly disappearing, the eastern bluebird will often choose a birdhouse for its nest. The male, with its sky-blue back and earthen red breast, is attracted to a birdhouse as a safe home for him and his mate, whose coloring is duller and grayer.

Redbreasted Bluebird

God Is Everywhere

Each time you look up in the sky
Or watch the fluffy clouds drift by,
Or feel the sunshine warm and bright
Or watch the dark turn into light,
Or hear a bluebird sweetly sing
Or see the winter turn to spring,
Or stop to pick a daffodil
Or gather violets on some hill,
Or touch a leaf or see a tree—

It's all God whispering, "This is Me.
Because I lived here long ago
So all of you might come to know
That I am Light and I am Love,
And though I'm now in heaven above,
I'm just as near to you as when
I lived on earth and talked with men."

Eastern Bluebird

Welcome

You are my friend,
  This is the house of friendship.
As my guest, will you partake of the joy
  of friendship with me?
For while you are here,
    friendship is your genial host,
      and the welcome that awaits you is from the heart.
When you go, may you not go alone, but may you
    take with you the warmth and beauty of friendship,
      and may you bring it back
        each time you come to visit
          this house of friendship.

Eastern Bluebird

A Prayer for Happiness

Whenever I'm discouraged
    and lost in deep despair,
I bundle all my troubles up
    and go to God in prayer.

Then I beseech Him earnestly
    to hear my humble plea
And tell me how to serve Him
    and do it gallantly.

And so I pray this little prayer
    and hope that He will show me
How I can bring more happiness
    to all the folks who know me,

And give me hope and courage,
    enough for every day,
And faith to light the darkness
    when I stumble on my way,

And love and understanding,
    enough to make me kind,
So I may judge all people
    with my heart and not my mind.

Cardinal

Consideration—Cardinal

How pleasing it is, when, by a clouded sky, the woods are rendered so dark, that were it not for an occasional glimpse of clearer light falling between the trees, you might imagine night at hand, while you are yet far distant from your home—how pleasing to have your ear suddenly saluted by the well known notes of this favorite bird, assuring you of peace around, and of the full hour that still remains for you to pursue your walk in security! How often have I enjoyed this pleasure, and how often, in due humbleness of hope, do I trust that I may enjoy it again.

Audubon

The cardinal is worthy of study for acts of consideration. The male is usually seen flying or perched with its mate and has been observed placing food tenderly in its mate's bill. The male also displays strong paternal instinct and assists in caring for the young.

Cardinal

Secrets of Creation
Belong to God Alone

In this restless world of struggle,
  it is very hard to find
Answers to the questions
  that daily come to mind.
Can we prove the endless wonder
  of the stars that shine at night?
Of the flowers that bloom in beauty
  and the birds in rhythmic flight?
Of the mountains in their grandeur
  and the rolling plains' wide sweep
Or the overwhelming wonder
  of a little child asleep?
We cannot see the future—
  what's beyond is still unknown,
For the secrets of creation
  still belong to God alone.

Cardinal

Spring Song

"The earth is the Lord's
   and the fullness thereof . . ."
It speaks of His greatness
   and sings of His love.
And the wonder and glory
   of the first Easter morn,
Like the first Christmas night
   when the Savior was born,
Are blended together
   in symphonic splendor
And God, with a voice
   that is gentle and tender,
Speaks to all hearts
   attuned to his voice,
Bidding His listeners
   to gladly rejoice,
For He that was born
   to be crucified
Arose from the grave
   to be glorified.
And the birds in the trees
   and the flowers of spring
All join in proclaiming
   this Heavenly King.

Cardinal

God Bless You
and Keep You in His Care

There are many things in life
we cannot understand,
But we must trust God's judgment
and be guided by His hand.
And all who have God's blessing
can rest safely in His care,
For He promises safe passage
on the wings of faith and prayer.

Mourning Dove

Peace—Dove

The Mourning Dove announces the approach of spring, and makes us forget the chilling blasts of winter by the soft melancholy of her cooing. Her heart is already so warmed and swollen by the ardor of her passion that it feels as ready to expand as do the buds on the trees beneath the genial sunshine. A man who had been a pirate once assured me, in the Florida Keys, that the soft, melancholy cry awoke feelings of repentance in his heart. . . . So moved was he by the notes of any bird—and especially those of a dove—that he finally decided to escape from his vessel, abandon his rough companions and return to his family.

Audubon (1835)

The mourning dove, a small pigeon, is thought to be the only bird that nests in all forty-eight contiguous states. Incubation of its eggs is shared by male and female: she during the day, and he at night. The ground dove, observed in gardens, on beaches, and in open fields, is considered one of the tamest of birds. The passenger pigeon, once possibly the most common bird in North America, became extinct by 1900.

33

Blue Ground Dove

I Come to Meet You

I come to meet You, God, and as I linger here
    I seem to feel You very near.
A rustling leaf, a rolling slope
    speak to my heart of endless hope.
The sun just rising in the sky,
    the waking birdlings as they fly,
The grass all wet with morning dew
    are telling me I just met You.
And, gently, thus the day is born
    as night gives way to breaking morn,
And once again I've met You, God,
    and worshipped on Your holy sod.
For who could see the dawn break through
    without a glimpse of heaven and You?
For who but God could make the day
    and softly put the night away?

Passenger Pigeon

Oh, for the Wings

Oh, for the wings of a bird we cry,
    to carry us off to an untroubled sky
Where we can dwell untouched by care
    and always be free as a bird in the air.
But there is a legend that's very old,
    not often heard and seldom told,
That once all birds were wingless, too,
    unable to soar through skies of blue.
They too were powerless to fly—
    until one day the Lord came by
And laid at the feet of the singing birds
    gossamer wings as He spoke these words,
"Come take these burdens, so heavy now,
    but if you bear them you'll learn somehow
That as you wear them they'll grow light
    and soon you can lift yourselves into flight."
So, folding the wings beneath their hearts
    and after endless failures and starts,
They lifted themselves and found with delight
    the wings that were heavy had grown so light.
So whenever you cry for the wings of a bird,
    remember this little legend you've heard
And let God give you a heart that sings
    as He turns your burdens to silver wings.

Broadbilled Hummingbird

Tenacity—Hummingbird

I hear the loud hum and see a splendid male hummingbird coming zigzag in long tacks, like a bee, but far swifter, along the edge of the swamp, in hot haste. He turns aside to taste the honey of the *Andromeda calyculata* (already visited by bees) within a rod of me. This golden-green gem. Its burnished back looks as if covered with green scales dusted with gold. It hovers, as it were stationary in the air, with an intense humming before each little flower-bell . . . and inserts its long tongue in each, turning toward me that splendid ruby on its breast, that glowing ruby.

Thoreau (1856)

The smallest known bird is the hummingbird; there are nearly 400 kinds ranging in size from the two-inch bee hummingbird to the eight-inch giant hummingbird. Transferring pollen from flower to flower, the hummingbird plays an integral role in the reproduction of plants.

Rufous Hummingbird

Where Can We Find Him?

The silent stars in timeless skies,
The wonderment in children's eyes,
The gossamer wings of a hummingbird,
The joy that comes from a kindly word,
The autumn haze, the breath of spring,
The chirping song the crickets sing,
A rosebud in a slender vase,
A smile upon a friendly face . . .

In everything both great and small
We see the hand of God in all,
And every day somewhere, someplace
We see the likeness of His face.
For who can watch a new day's birth
Or touch the warm life-giving earth
And say they've never seen His face
Or looked upon His throne of grace?

Ruby-throated Hummingbird

Hidden in the Heart

Thoughts of love and gratitude
   are fragile, cherished things
As gossamer as fleecy clouds
   or hummingbirds' small wings,
And often through the passing days
   we feel down deep inside
Unspoken thoughts of thankfulness
   and fond, admiring pride.
But words can say so little
   when the heart is overflowing,
And often those we love the most
   just have no way of knowing
The many things the heart conceals
   and never can impart,
For words seem so inadequate
   to express what's in the heart.

Great Horned Owl

Wisdom—Owl

*H*ow often when snugly settled under the boughs of my temporary encampment, and preparing to roast a venison steak of the body of a squirrel, have I been saluted with the exulting bursts of this nightly disturber of the peace. How often have I seen this nocturnal marauder alight within a few yards of me, expose his whole body to the glare of my fire, and eye me in such a curious manner that, had it been reasonable to do so, I would gladly have invited him to join me in my repast . . . his society would be at least as agreeable as that of many of the buffoons we meet in the world.

Audubon

The eyes of most birds are situated on the sides of the head and provide a wide field of vision, but the eyes of owls face forward, affording them the precise perception necessary to strike at quick-moving prey. Many owls have a wide ring of feathers around each eye, giving them a studious appearance, and thus, the expression "wise old owl."

Homestead Screech Owl

Wisdom

Father, I have knowledge,
   so will You show me now
How to use it wisely
   and to find a way somehow
To make the world I live in
   a little better place
And to make life with its problems
   a bit easier to face?

Grant me faith and courage,
   put purpose in my days,
And show me how to serve Thee
   in the most effective ways,
So all my education,
   my knowledge and my skill
May find their true fulfillment
   as I learn to do Thy will.

And may I ever be aware
   in everything I do
That knowledge comes from learning,
   and wisdom comes from You.

Snowy Owl

Be Wise

Sometimes the things that seem the worst
    turn out to be the best,
And this is just a signal
    that you need a little rest.
For while we cannot understand
    why things happen as they do,
The One who hangs the rainbow out
    has His own plans for you.
And when the dark days come
    and we cannot understand,
We must trust His wisdom
    and be guided by His hand.
And may it comfort you to know
    that you are in His care,
For we are all a part of God
    and God is everywhere.

Barred Owl

Climb Till Your Dream Comes True

Often your tasks will be many,
  and more than you think you can do.
Often the road will be rugged,
  and the hills insurmountable, too.

But always remember, the hills ahead
  are never as steep as they seem,
And with faith in your heart, start upward
  and climb till you reach your dream.

For nothing in life that is worthy
  is ever too hard to achieve
If you have the courage to try it
  and you have the faith to believe.

For faith is a force that is greater
  than knowledge or power or skill,
And many defeats turn to triumphs
  if you trust in God's wisdom and will.

For faith is a mover of mountains—
  there's nothing that God cannot do—
So start out today with faith in your heart
  and climb till your dream comes true.

Snowy Owl

His Way

Knowledge comes from learning,
    but wisdom comes from God,
The God that made the universe—
    the sea, the sky, the sod—
The God who makes it possible
    to find miracles each day,
If we but trust His wisdom
    and follow in His way.

Robin

Tenderness—Robin

The robin is one's constant companion. When the day is sunny and the ground bare, you meet him at all points and hear him at all hours. At sunset, on the tops of the tall maples, with look heavenward, and in a spirit of utter abandonment, he carols his simple strain. And sitting thus amid the stark, silent reeds, above the wet, cold earth, with the chill of winter still in the air, there is no fitter or sweeter songster in the whole round year. It is in keeping with the scene and the occasion. How round and genuine the notes are, and how eagerly our ears drink them all in! The first utterance, and the spell of winter is thoroughly broken and the remembrance of it afar off.

John Burroughs (1895)

Legend has it that the robin's breast became red because one night long ago, a robin continued to fly over and fan the embers of a smoldering campfire to keep some small children warm when they were lost in the forest. A harbinger of spring, the robin has such refined, sensitive hearing it can hear the movement of earthworms underground.

Robin

All Things Pass

Let all your thoughts be happy, dear,
To chase away all thoughts of fear.
Think of lovely things you've seen
Like rolling slopes of velvet green,
Fluffy clouds of azure blue,
Sparkling drops of crystal dew,
Robin redbreasts on the wing
Telling us again it's spring,
Golden beds of daffodils,
Violets blooming on a hill.
Don't cloud your mind with anxious fear—
Just fill your heart with sunny cheer
And waiting days will soon be over
And you'll again be back in clover
For all things pass and this will, too,
And with God's help you'll come smiling through.

Robin

When Robins Start to Sing

No matter how downhearted
    and discouraged we may be,
New hope is born when we behold
    leaves budding on a tree,
And troubles seem to vanish
    when robins start to sing,
For God never sends the winter
    without the joy of spring.

Robin

Wings of Prayer

Just close your eyes and open your heart
And feel your cares and worries depart.
Just yield yourself to the Father above
And let Him hold you secure in His love.
For life on earth grows more involved
With endless problems that can't be solved,
But God only asks us to do our best
Then He will take over and finish the rest.
So when you are tired, discouraged, and blue,
There's always one door that is opened to you
And that is the door to the house of prayer,
And you'll find God waiting to meet you there.
And the house of prayer is no farther away
Than the quiet spot where you kneel and pray,
For the heart is a temple when God is there
As we place ourselves in His loving care.
And He hears every prayer and answers each one
When we pray in His name, "Thy will be done."
And the burdens that seemed too heavy to bear
Are lifted away on the wings of prayer.

Robin

The Tenderness of Friendship

Nothing on earth can
    make life more worthwhile
Than a true, loyal friend
    and the warmth of a smile,
For, just like a sunbeam
    makes cloudy days brighter,
The smile of a friend
    makes a heavy heart lighter.

Chestnut-sided Warbler, Parula Warbler, Black-throated Warbler, Prothonotary Warbler

Joy—Songbird

Witness the clear, sweet whistle of the gray-crested titmouse—the soft, nasal piping of the nuthatch—the amorous, vivacious warble of the bluebird—the long, rich note of the meadow-lark—the whistle of the quail—the drumming of the partridge—the animation and loquacity of the swallows, and the like. Even the hen has a homely, contented carol; and I credit the owls with a desire to fill the night with music. All birds are incipient or would-be songsters in the spring. I find corrob-orative evidence of this even in the crowing of the cock. The flowering of the maple is not so obvious as that of the magnolia; nevertheless, there is actual inflorescence.

John Burroughs (1895)

There are approximately 8600 kinds of birds in the world, and each species has its individual, identifiable song. Warblers, small birds with thin bills, have a repertoire of complex and melodious songs.

House Wren

Believe

When the way seems long
  and the day is dark
And we can't hear the sound
  of the thrush or the lark,
That is the time
  when faith alone
Can lead us
  out of the dark unknown.
For faith to believe
  when the way is rough
And faith to hang on
  when the going is tough
Will never fail
  to pull us through
And bring us strength
  and comfort, too.
For all we really
  ever need
Is faith
  as a grain of mustard seed,
For all God asks is
  do you believe—
For if you do
  you shall receive.

Eastern Meadowlark

Trust the Father

Do not be anxious, said our Lord,
   have peace from day to day—
The lilies neither toil nor spin,
   yet none are clothed as they.
The meadowlark with sweetest song
   fears not for bread or nest
Because he trusts our Father's love
   and God knows what is best.

Goldfinch

Meet God in the Morning

Each day at dawning,
   I lift my heart high
And raise up my eyes
   to the infinite sky.
I watch the night vanish
   as a new day is born,
And I hear the birds sing
   on the wings of the morn.
I see the dew glisten
   in crystal-like splendor
While God, with a touch
   that is gentle and tender,
Wraps up the night
   and softly tucks it away
And hangs out the sun
   to herald a new day.
And so I give thanks
   and my heart kneels to pray,
"God, keep me and guide me
   and go with me today."

Goldfinch

Brighten the Corner Where You Are

We cannot all be famous or listed in "Who's Who,"
But every person, great or small, has important work to do,
For seldom do we realize the importance of small deeds
Or to what degree of greatness unnoticed kindness leads.

For it's not the big celebrity in a world of fame and praise,
But it's doing unpretentiously in indistinguished ways
The work that God assigned to us, unimportant as it seems,
That makes our task outstanding and brings reality to dreams.

So do not sit and idly wish for wider, new dimensions
Where you can put in practice your many good intentions,
But at the spot God placed you, begin at once to do
Little things to brighten up the lives surrounding you.

For if everybody brightened up the spot on which they're standing
By being more considerate and a little less demanding,
This dark old world would very soon eclipse the evening star,
If everybody brightened up the corner where they are.

Indigo Buntings

The Beauty of Spring

God lives in the beauty
    that comes with spring—
The colorful flowers,
    the birds that sing,
And He lives in people
    as kind as you,
And He lives in all
    the nice things you do.

North American Redheaded Woodpecker

Perseverance—Woodpecker

*A*h! There is the note—a prolonged monotonous wick-wick-quick-quick-quick, etc., or, if you please, quick-quick, heard far over and through the dry leaves. But how that single sound peoples and enriches all the woods and fields! It is as when a family, your neighbors, return to an empty house after a long absence, and you hear the cheerful hum of voices and laughter of children, and see the smoke from the kitchen fire. The doors are thrown open, and children go screaming through the hall. So the flicker [woodpecker] dashes through the aisles of the grove, throws up a window here and cackles out it, and then there, airing the house. It makes its voice ring upstairs and downstairs, and so, as it were, fits it for its habitation and ours, and takes possession. It is as good as a housewarming to all nature.

Thoreau (1858)

The woodpecker's chisel-like beak is designed for chipping bark, investigating dead tree trunks for larvae, and excavating nest holes. Its skull is designed to absorb and take the strain of prolonged hammering. Woodpeckers have stiff, spiny tails that act as props as they make their way up trees.

Downy Woodpecker

When Troubles Assail You

When life seems empty
and there's no place to go,
When your heart is troubled
and your spirits are low,
When friends seem few
and nobody cares—
There is always God
to hear your prayer.
And whatever you're facing
will seem much less
When you go to God
and confide and confess,
For the burden that seems
too heavy to bear
God lifts away
on the wings of prayer.
So go to our Father
when troubles assail you,
For His grace is sufficient
and He'll never fail you.

Redheaded Woodpecker

Adversity Can Distress Us or Bless Us

The way we use adversity
    is strictly our own choice,
For in God's hands
    adversity can make the heart rejoice.
For everything God sends to us,
    no matter in what form,
Is sent with plan and purpose,
    for by the fierceness of a storm
The atmosphere is changed and cleared
    and the earth is washed and clean,
And the high winds of adversity
    can make restless souls serene.
And while it's very difficult
    for mankind to understand
God's intentions and His purpose
    and the workings of His hand,
If we observe the miracles
    that happen every day,
We cannot help but be convinced
    that in His wondrous way
God makes what seemed unbearable
    and painful and distressing
Easily acceptable
    when we view it as a blessing.

Ivory-billed Woodpecker

Stepping-stones to God

An aching heart is but a stepping-stone
To greater joy than you've ever known,
For things that cause the heart to ache
Until you think that it must break
Become the strength by which we climb
To higher heights that are sublime
And feel the radiance of God's smiles
When we have soared above life's trials.
So when you're overwhelmed with fears
And all your hopes are drenched in tears,
Think not that life has been unfair
And given you too much to bear,
For God has chosen you because,
With all your weaknesses and flaws,
He feels that you are worthy of
The greatness of His wondrous love.
So welcome every stumbling block
And every thorn and jagged rock,
For each one is a stepping-stone
To God, who wants you for His own.
And as you grow in strength and grace
The clearer you can see God's face,
And on the stepping-stones of strife
You reach at last eternal life.

Bobwhite Quail

Wings of Encouragement

Therefore I tell you, do not worry about your life, what you will eat or drink; or about your body, what you will wear. Is not life more important than food, and the body more important than clothes? Look at the birds of the air; they do not sow or reap or store away in barns, and yet your heavenly Father feeds them. Are you not much more valuable than they? Who of you by worrying can add a single hour to his life?

Matthew 6:25–27 NIV

The bobwhite quail nests on the ground in dense cover; the female can lay as many as twenty eggs. Quail form winter flocks known as coveys. Quail roost in a circle, each facing outward, to permit a hasty exit if a predator approaches.

Two Palestinian Seas

A very favorite story of mine
   is about two seas in Palestine.
One is a sparkling, sapphire jewel—
   its waters are clean and clear and cool.
Along its shores the children play
   and travelers seek it on their way,
And nature gives so lavishly
   her choicest gems to the Galilee.
But on the south, the Jordan flows
   into a sea where nothing grows.
No splash of fish, no singing bird,
   no children's laughter is ever heard.
The air hangs heavy all around,
   and nature shuns this barren ground.
Both seas receive the Jordan's flow—
   the water is just the same, we know—
But one of the seas, like liquid sun,
   can warm the hearts of everyone,
While, farther south, another sea
   is dead and dark and miserly.

It takes each drop the Jordan brings
    and to each drop it fiercely clings.
It hoards and holds the Jordan's waves
    until the captured, shackled slaves
The fresh, clear Jordan turns to salt
    to die within the Dead Sea's vault.
But the Jordan flows on rapturously
    as it enters and leaves the Galilee,
For every drop the Jordan gives
    becomes a laughing wave that lives,
For the Galilee gives back each drop—
    its waters flow and never stop.
And in this laughing, living sea
    that takes and gives so generously,
We find the way to live and living
    is not in keeping but in giving.
Yes, there are two Palestine seas,
    and mankind is fashioned after these.

Tern

Hawk

One Thing Never Changes

The seasons swiftly come and go,
    and with them comes the thought
Of all the various changes
    that time in flight has brought.
But one thing never changes,
    it remains the same forever.
God truly loves His children
    and He will forsake them never.

Snow Goose, Blue Goose

The Gift of Lasting Love

Love is much more than a tender caress
And more than hours of bright happiness,
For a lasting love is made up of sharing
Both hours that are joyous and also despairing.
It's made up of patience and deep understanding
And never of stubborn or selfish demanding.
It's made up of climbing the steep hills together
And facing with courage life's stormiest weather.
And nothing on earth or in heaven can part
A love that has grown to be part of the heart,
And just like the sun and the stars and the sea,
This love will go on through eternity.
True love lives on when earthly things die,
For it's part of the spirit that soars to the sky.

Golden Eagle

Can Happiness Be Captured?

Across the years, we've met in dreams
And shared each other's hopes and schemes.
We've known a friendship rich and rare
And beautiful beyond compare.
Still, you reached out your arms for more
To catch what you were yearning for,
But little did you think or guess
That one can't capture happiness
Because it's unrestrained and free,
Unfettered by reality.

Trumpeter Swan

Take Courage

It's easy to grow downhearted
    when nothing goes your way.
It's easy to be discouraged
    when you have a troublesome day.
But trouble is only a challenge
    to spur you on to achieve
The best that God has to offer,
    if you have the faith to believe!